# 50 Farm-Fresh Egg Recipes for Home

By: Kelly Johnson

## Table of Contents

- Classic Deviled Eggs
- Shakshuka with Feta
- Spanish Tortilla
- Egg and Asparagus Salad
- Egg Drop Soup
- Spinach and Feta Omelette
- Quiche Lorraine
- Eggs Benedict
- Cloud Eggs
- Huevos Rancheros
- Baked Eggs with Tomatoes and Feta
- Egg Salad Sandwiches
- Mushroom and Swiss Cheese Frittata
- Egg Curry
- Smoked Salmon and Cream Cheese Scramble
- Egg and Cheese Breakfast Burritos
- Fried Rice with Eggs and Vegetables
- Sweet Potato and Egg Hash
- Veggie-Packed Egg Muffins
- Poached Eggs on Avocado Toast
- Egg and Bacon Breakfast Casserole
- Green Shakshuka
- Creamy Garlic Mashed Potatoes with Poached Egg
- Spinach and Egg Breakfast Wrap
- Sweet Corn Fritters with Egg
- Savory Dutch Baby Pancake with Eggs
- Classic Egg Fried Rice
- Tomato Basil Egg Bake
- Egg and Vegetable Stir-Fry
- Eggs in Purgatory

- Breakfast Egg Quesadilla
- Egg and Cheese Scones
- Broccoli and Cheddar Quiche
- Egg and Potato Breakfast Skillet
- Mediterranean Egg Bake
- Egg-Stuffed Bell Peppers
- Spinach, Bacon, and Egg Salad
- Crispy Eggplant and Egg Sandwich
- Caprese Egg Bake
- Bacon-Wrapped Eggs
- Frittata with Roasted Vegetables
- Egg Tacos with Salsa Verde
- Egg and Cheese Breakfast Bowl
- Tomato and Egg Stir-Fry
- Egg and Quinoa Breakfast Bowl
- Herb-Crusted Baked Eggs
- Korean Gyeran-jjim (Steamed Eggs)
- Eggs with Ratatouille
- Cauliflower and Egg Casserole
- Rustic Egg and Vegetable Tart

**Classic Deviled Eggs**

**Ingredients:**

- 6 large eggs
- 3 tablespoons mayonnaise
- 1 teaspoon Dijon mustard (or yellow mustard)
- 1 teaspoon white vinegar
- Salt and pepper to taste
- Paprika, for garnish
- Fresh chives or parsley, for garnish (optional)

**Instructions:**

1. **Boil the Eggs**:
    - Place the eggs in a single layer in a saucepan and cover them with water.
    - Bring the water to a boil over medium-high heat. Once boiling, cover the pan, remove it from heat, and let it sit for 9-12 minutes (9 minutes for slightly soft yolks, 12 minutes for fully hard yolks).
2. **Cool the Eggs**:
    - Transfer the eggs to a bowl of ice water to cool for about 5 minutes. This makes peeling easier.
3. **Peel the Eggs**:
    - Gently tap the eggs on a hard surface to crack the shell, then peel under running water.
4. **Prepare the Filling**:
    - Slice the eggs in half lengthwise and remove the yolks, placing them in a mixing bowl.
    - Mash the yolks with a fork, then add mayonnaise, Dijon mustard, white vinegar, salt, and pepper. Mix until smooth and creamy.
5. **Fill the Egg Whites**:
    - Spoon or pipe the yolk mixture back into the egg whites.
6. **Garnish and Serve**:
    - Sprinkle paprika on top for color and flavor. If desired, add chopped chives or parsley for garnish.
    - Serve immediately or refrigerate until ready to serve.

Enjoy your classic deviled eggs!

## Shakshuka with Feta

**Ingredients:**

- 2 tablespoons olive oil
- 1 onion, diced
- 1 bell pepper, diced
- 3 cloves garlic, minced
- 1 teaspoon ground cumin
- 1 teaspoon paprika
- 1 can (14 oz) diced tomatoes
- 4 large eggs
- Salt and pepper to taste
- 1/2 cup feta cheese, crumbled
- Fresh parsley, for garnish

**Instructions:**

1. Heat olive oil in a skillet over medium heat. Add onion and bell pepper, cooking until softened.
2. Stir in garlic, cumin, and paprika, cooking for another minute.
3. Add diced tomatoes and simmer for 10 minutes, seasoning with salt and pepper.
4. Create small wells in the sauce and crack an egg into each well. Cover and cook until the eggs are set.
5. Sprinkle feta cheese on top and garnish with fresh parsley before serving.

## Spanish Tortilla

**Ingredients:**

- 4 large eggs
- 2 medium potatoes, thinly sliced
- 1 onion, thinly sliced
- Olive oil
- Salt and pepper to taste

**Instructions:**

1. Heat olive oil in a skillet over medium heat. Add potatoes and onion, cooking until tender.
2. In a bowl, beat the eggs and season with salt and pepper.
3. Drain excess oil from the potato mixture and combine with the eggs.
4. Return the mixture to the skillet, cooking until set on the bottom. Flip and cook the other side until golden.
5. Serve warm or at room temperature, cut into wedges.

**Egg and Asparagus Salad**

**Ingredients:**

- 4 hard-boiled eggs, chopped
- 1 bunch asparagus, trimmed and blanched
- 2 tablespoons mayonnaise
- 1 tablespoon Dijon mustard
- Salt and pepper to taste
- Fresh dill or chives, for garnish

**Instructions:**

1. In a large bowl, combine chopped eggs and blanched asparagus.
2. In a small bowl, mix mayonnaise, Dijon mustard, salt, and pepper.
3. Gently fold the dressing into the egg and asparagus mixture.
4. Garnish with fresh dill or chives and serve chilled.

**Egg Drop Soup**

**Ingredients:**

- 4 cups chicken broth
- 2 large eggs
- 1 tablespoon cornstarch mixed with 2 tablespoons water
- 1 green onion, chopped
- Salt and pepper to taste

**Instructions:**

1. Bring chicken broth to a simmer in a pot.
2. Stir in the cornstarch mixture and simmer until thickened.
3. Beat the eggs and slowly pour into the broth, stirring gently to create ribbons.
4. Season with salt and pepper, and garnish with chopped green onion before serving.

## Spinach and Feta Omelette

**Ingredients:**

- 3 large eggs
- 1 cup fresh spinach, chopped
- 1/2 cup feta cheese, crumbled
- 1 tablespoon olive oil
- Salt and pepper to taste

**Instructions:**

1. Heat olive oil in a skillet over medium heat. Add spinach and sauté until wilted.
2. In a bowl, beat eggs with salt and pepper. Pour the eggs over the spinach.
3. Cook until the eggs are set, then sprinkle feta cheese on one half.
4. Fold the omelette in half and serve warm.

## Quiche Lorraine

**Ingredients:**

- 1 pie crust (store-bought or homemade)
- 6 large eggs
- 1 cup heavy cream
- 1 cup cooked bacon, chopped
- 1 cup shredded Swiss cheese
- Salt and pepper to taste

**Instructions:**

1. Preheat oven to 375°F (190°C).
2. Place the pie crust in a pie dish and pre-bake for 10 minutes.
3. In a bowl, whisk together eggs, heavy cream, salt, and pepper.
4. Layer bacon and cheese in the crust, then pour the egg mixture on top.
5. Bake for 35-40 minutes, until the quiche is set and lightly browned. Allow to cool slightly before slicing.

## Eggs Benedict

**Ingredients:**

- 2 English muffins, split
- 4 large eggs
- 2 tablespoons white vinegar
- 4 slices Canadian bacon
- 1/2 cup hollandaise sauce (store-bought or homemade)
- Fresh chives, for garnish

**Instructions:**

1. Toast the English muffins and keep warm.
2. In a pot, bring water and vinegar to a simmer. Crack eggs into individual cups and gently slide them into the water. Poach for about 3 minutes until the whites are set.
3. In a skillet, heat the Canadian bacon until warmed through.
4. To assemble, place a slice of Canadian bacon on each muffin half, top with a poached egg, and drizzle with hollandaise sauce.
5. Garnish with chopped chives and serve immediately.

Enjoy these delicious egg dishes!

**Cloud Eggs**

**Ingredients:**

- 4 large eggs
- Salt and pepper to taste
- Fresh herbs (chives, parsley, or thyme) for garnish

**Instructions:**

1. Preheat the oven to 375°F (190°C) and line a baking sheet with parchment paper.
2. Separate the egg whites from the yolks, placing the whites in a mixing bowl and the yolks in separate small bowls.
3. Beat the egg whites with a mixer until stiff peaks form. Season with salt and pepper.
4. Spoon the whipped egg whites onto the baking sheet, creating a nest shape with a small well in the center for the yolk.
5. Bake for 3-4 minutes, then carefully place a yolk in each well and bake for an additional 3-5 minutes, until the yolks are slightly set.
6. Garnish with fresh herbs before serving.

**Huevos Rancheros**

**Ingredients:**

- 4 large eggs
- 2 corn tortillas
- 1 cup refried beans (canned or homemade)
- 1 cup salsa (homemade or store-bought)
- 1 avocado, sliced
- Fresh cilantro for garnish
- Salt and pepper to taste

**Instructions:**

1. Heat the refried beans in a saucepan over medium heat.
2. In a separate skillet, fry the tortillas until lightly crispy.
3. In the same skillet, fry the eggs sunny-side up, seasoning with salt and pepper.
4. To assemble, spread refried beans on each tortilla, top with a fried egg, and spoon salsa over the top.
5. Garnish with avocado slices and fresh cilantro before serving.

## Baked Eggs with Tomatoes and Feta

**Ingredients:**

- 4 large eggs
- 1 can (14 oz) diced tomatoes, drained
- 1/2 cup feta cheese, crumbled
- 2 tablespoons olive oil
- 1 teaspoon dried oregano
- Salt and pepper to taste

**Instructions:**

1. Preheat the oven to 375°F (190°C) and grease a baking dish.
2. Spread the diced tomatoes in the bottom of the dish and drizzle with olive oil. Season with oregano, salt, and pepper.
3. Make 4 wells in the tomato mixture and crack an egg into each well.
4. Sprinkle feta cheese over the top and bake for 20-25 minutes, until the eggs are set.
5. Serve warm with crusty bread.

**Egg Salad Sandwiches**

**Ingredients:**

- 6 hard-boiled eggs, chopped
- 1/4 cup mayonnaise
- 1 teaspoon Dijon mustard
- Salt and pepper to taste
- 1/4 cup celery, diced
- 1/4 cup green onion, sliced
- Bread or lettuce leaves for serving

**Instructions:**

1. In a bowl, combine chopped eggs, mayonnaise, Dijon mustard, celery, green onion, salt, and pepper.
2. Mix until well combined.
3. Serve on bread as a sandwich or in lettuce leaves for a lighter option.

## Mushroom and Swiss Cheese Frittata

**Ingredients:**

- 6 large eggs
- 1 cup mushrooms, sliced
- 1/2 cup Swiss cheese, shredded
- 1/4 cup milk
- 1 tablespoon olive oil
- Salt and pepper to taste

**Instructions:**

1. Preheat the oven to 375°F (190°C).
2. Heat olive oil in an oven-safe skillet over medium heat. Sauté mushrooms until tender.
3. In a bowl, whisk together eggs, milk, salt, and pepper. Pour the mixture over the mushrooms.
4. Cook on the stovetop for 2-3 minutes until the edges start to set, then sprinkle Swiss cheese on top.
5. Transfer the skillet to the oven and bake for 15-20 minutes, until the frittata is fully set. Slice and serve warm.

# Egg Curry

**Ingredients:**

- 6 hard-boiled eggs, peeled
- 1 onion, diced
- 2 tomatoes, chopped
- 2 tablespoons curry powder
- 1 cup coconut milk
- 2 tablespoons vegetable oil
- Salt and pepper to taste

**Instructions:**

1. Heat vegetable oil in a skillet over medium heat. Add diced onion and sauté until golden.
2. Stir in chopped tomatoes and cook until soft. Add curry powder and cook for another minute.
3. Pour in coconut milk, bringing the mixture to a simmer. Season with salt and pepper.
4. Add the hard-boiled eggs to the sauce, simmering for 5-10 minutes. Serve hot with rice or bread.

## Smoked Salmon and Cream Cheese Scramble

**Ingredients:**

- 4 large eggs
- 1/4 cup cream cheese
- 1/2 cup smoked salmon, chopped
- 1 tablespoon chives, chopped
- Salt and pepper to taste
- 1 tablespoon butter

**Instructions:**

1. In a bowl, whisk together eggs, cream cheese, salt, and pepper until well combined.
2. Heat butter in a skillet over medium heat. Pour in the egg mixture, stirring gently.
3. When the eggs start to set, add the chopped smoked salmon and chives. Continue cooking until the eggs are fully set.
4. Serve warm with toast or bagels.

Enjoy these delicious egg dishes!

## Egg and Cheese Breakfast Burritos

**Ingredients:**

- 4 large eggs
- 1/2 cup shredded cheese (cheddar or your choice)
- 1/2 cup cooked breakfast sausage or diced ham (optional)
- 4 large flour tortillas
- 1/4 cup milk
- Salt and pepper to taste
- Salsa for serving

**Instructions:**

1. In a bowl, whisk together eggs, milk, salt, and pepper.
2. Heat a skillet over medium heat and scramble the egg mixture until fully cooked.
3. Add cheese and sausage or ham (if using), stirring until the cheese melts.
4. Place a portion of the egg mixture in the center of each tortilla, fold in the sides, and roll up tightly.
5. Serve with salsa on the side.

## Fried Rice with Eggs and Vegetables

**Ingredients:**

- 2 cups cooked rice (preferably day-old)
- 2 large eggs, beaten
- 1 cup mixed vegetables (carrots, peas, bell peppers)
- 2 tablespoons soy sauce
- 1 tablespoon sesame oil
- 2 green onions, chopped
- Salt and pepper to taste

**Instructions:**

1. Heat sesame oil in a large skillet or wok over medium-high heat.
2. Add mixed vegetables and stir-fry for a few minutes until tender.
3. Push the vegetables to the side and pour the beaten eggs into the skillet, scrambling until cooked.
4. Add the cooked rice and soy sauce, mixing everything together.
5. Season with salt and pepper, and garnish with chopped green onions before serving.

## Sweet Potato and Egg Hash

**Ingredients:**

- 2 medium sweet potatoes, diced
- 4 large eggs
- 1 bell pepper, diced
- 1 small onion, diced
- 2 tablespoons olive oil
- Salt and pepper to taste

**Instructions:**

1. Heat olive oil in a large skillet over medium heat. Add diced sweet potatoes and cook until tender, about 10-15 minutes.
2. Add onion and bell pepper, cooking until softened. Season with salt and pepper.
3. Create four wells in the hash and crack an egg into each well. Cover and cook until the eggs are set to your liking.
4. Serve hot, garnished with fresh herbs if desired.

**Veggie-Packed Egg Muffins**

**Ingredients:**

- 6 large eggs
- 1/2 cup milk
- 1 cup mixed vegetables (spinach, bell peppers, tomatoes)
- 1/2 cup cheese (cheddar or your choice), shredded
- Salt and pepper to taste

**Instructions:**

1. Preheat the oven to 350°F (175°C) and grease a muffin tin.
2. In a bowl, whisk together eggs, milk, salt, and pepper.
3. Add mixed vegetables and cheese, stirring to combine.
4. Pour the egg mixture into the muffin tin, filling each cup about 2/3 full.
5. Bake for 20-25 minutes, until the egg muffins are set and slightly golden. Allow to cool before removing from the tin.

## Poached Eggs on Avocado Toast

**Ingredients:**

- 2 slices of bread (whole grain or your choice)
- 1 ripe avocado, mashed
- 2 large eggs
- Salt and pepper to taste
- Red pepper flakes (optional)
- Fresh lemon juice (optional)

**Instructions:**

1. Toast the bread slices until golden brown.
2. In a saucepan, bring water to a simmer and add a splash of vinegar. Crack the eggs into small bowls and gently slide them into the simmering water. Poach for about 3-4 minutes until the whites are set.
3. Spread mashed avocado on each slice of toast, seasoning with salt, pepper, and red pepper flakes if desired.
4. Top each toast with a poached egg and a squeeze of lemon juice before serving.

**Egg and Bacon Breakfast Casserole**

**Ingredients:**

- 6 large eggs
- 1 cup milk
- 1 cup cooked bacon, chopped
- 2 cups cubed bread
- 1 cup shredded cheese (cheddar or your choice)
- Salt and pepper to taste

**Instructions:**

1. Preheat the oven to 350°F (175°C) and grease a baking dish.
2. In a bowl, whisk together eggs, milk, salt, and pepper.
3. Layer the cubed bread, chopped bacon, and cheese in the baking dish.
4. Pour the egg mixture over the top, pressing down slightly to ensure everything is soaked.
5. Bake for 30-35 minutes, until the casserole is set and golden on top. Allow to cool slightly before slicing.

**Green Shakshuka**

**Ingredients:**

- 2 tablespoons olive oil
- 1 onion, diced
- 2 cups spinach, chopped
- 1 cup kale, chopped
- 1 cup parsley or cilantro, chopped
- 4 large eggs
- Salt and pepper to taste
- Feta cheese, for garnish (optional)

**Instructions:**

1. Heat olive oil in a skillet over medium heat. Add onion and sauté until translucent.
2. Stir in spinach, kale, and parsley or cilantro, cooking until wilted. Season with salt and pepper.
3. Create wells in the greens and crack an egg into each well. Cover and cook until the eggs are set.
4. Garnish with feta cheese if desired and serve warm with crusty bread.

Enjoy these delicious egg dishes!

**Creamy Garlic Mashed Potatoes with Poached Egg**

**Ingredients:**

- 2 pounds potatoes, peeled and diced
- 4 cloves garlic, minced
- 1/2 cup heavy cream
- 4 tablespoons butter
- Salt and pepper to taste
- 4 large eggs
- Fresh chives for garnish

**Instructions:**

1. Boil the diced potatoes in salted water until tender, about 15-20 minutes. Drain and return to the pot.
2. Add minced garlic, heavy cream, butter, salt, and pepper to the potatoes. Mash until smooth and creamy.
3. In a separate pot, bring water to a simmer and poach the eggs for 3-4 minutes until the whites are set.
4. Serve the creamy mashed potatoes topped with a poached egg and garnish with fresh chives.

## Spinach and Egg Breakfast Wrap

**Ingredients:**

- 4 large eggs
- 1 cup fresh spinach, chopped
- 1/4 cup cheese (cheddar or feta), shredded
- 4 large tortillas
- Salt and pepper to taste
- Olive oil for cooking

**Instructions:**

1. In a skillet, heat olive oil over medium heat. Add spinach and cook until wilted.
2. In a bowl, whisk together eggs, salt, and pepper. Pour the mixture into the skillet with spinach and scramble until cooked.
3. Place a portion of the egg mixture on each tortilla, sprinkle with cheese, and roll them up.
4. Serve warm, optionally with salsa on the side.

**Sweet Corn Fritters with Egg**

**Ingredients:**

- 1 cup corn kernels (fresh or canned)
- 1/2 cup flour
- 2 large eggs
- 1/4 cup green onions, chopped
- 1/4 teaspoon baking powder
- Salt and pepper to taste
- Olive oil for frying

**Instructions:**

1. In a bowl, combine corn, flour, eggs, green onions, baking powder, salt, and pepper until well mixed.
2. Heat olive oil in a skillet over medium heat. Drop spoonfuls of the corn mixture into the skillet and flatten slightly.
3. Cook for 3-4 minutes on each side until golden brown.
4. Serve warm, optionally topped with a fried or poached egg.

**Savory Dutch Baby Pancake with Eggs**

**Ingredients:**

- 3 large eggs
- 3/4 cup milk
- 3/4 cup flour
- 1/2 teaspoon salt
- 2 tablespoons butter
- Toppings: cooked bacon or sausage, cheese, and fresh herbs

**Instructions:**

1. Preheat the oven to 425°F (220°C). In a blender, combine eggs, milk, flour, and salt, blending until smooth.
2. In a cast-iron skillet, melt butter over medium heat. Pour the batter into the skillet and transfer to the oven.
3. Bake for 20-25 minutes until puffed and golden.
4. Top with cooked bacon or sausage, cheese, and herbs before serving.

## Classic Egg Fried Rice

**Ingredients:**

- 2 cups cooked rice (preferably day-old)
- 2 large eggs, beaten
- 1 cup mixed vegetables (peas, carrots, bell peppers)
- 3 tablespoons soy sauce
- 2 tablespoons vegetable oil
- Green onions for garnish

**Instructions:**

1. Heat vegetable oil in a large skillet or wok over medium-high heat.
2. Add mixed vegetables and stir-fry for a few minutes until tender.
3. Push the vegetables to the side and pour in the beaten eggs, scrambling until cooked.
4. Add the cooked rice and soy sauce, mixing everything together.
5. Garnish with chopped green onions before serving.

**Tomato Basil Egg Bake**

**Ingredients:**

- 6 large eggs
- 1 cup cherry tomatoes, halved
- 1/2 cup fresh basil, chopped
- 1/2 cup cheese (mozzarella or your choice), shredded
- Salt and pepper to taste
- Olive oil for greasing

**Instructions:**

1. Preheat the oven to 375°F (190°C) and grease a baking dish.
2. In a bowl, whisk together eggs, salt, and pepper. Stir in cherry tomatoes, basil, and cheese.
3. Pour the egg mixture into the baking dish and bake for 25-30 minutes until set and lightly golden.
4. Allow to cool slightly before slicing and serving.

**Egg and Vegetable Stir-Fry**

**Ingredients:**

- 4 large eggs, beaten
- 2 cups mixed vegetables (bell peppers, broccoli, carrots)
- 2 tablespoons soy sauce
- 1 tablespoon sesame oil
- Salt and pepper to taste
- Green onions for garnish

**Instructions:**

1. Heat sesame oil in a large skillet over medium-high heat.
2. Add mixed vegetables and stir-fry until tender.
3. Push the vegetables to the side and pour the beaten eggs into the skillet, scrambling until cooked.
4. Add soy sauce, mixing everything together, and season with salt and pepper.
5. Garnish with chopped green onions before serving.

Enjoy these delicious egg dishes!

**Eggs in Purgatory**

**Ingredients:**

- 4 large eggs
- 1 can (15 oz) crushed tomatoes
- 2 cloves garlic, minced
- 1 teaspoon red pepper flakes (optional)
- 1 teaspoon olive oil
- Salt and pepper to taste
- Fresh basil or parsley for garnish
- Crusty bread for serving

**Instructions:**

1. Heat olive oil in a skillet over medium heat. Add garlic and red pepper flakes, cooking for 1-2 minutes until fragrant.
2. Stir in crushed tomatoes, seasoning with salt and pepper. Simmer for 5-10 minutes.
3. Make wells in the tomato sauce and crack an egg into each well. Cover and cook for 5-7 minutes until the eggs are set.
4. Garnish with fresh herbs and serve with crusty bread.

## Breakfast Egg Quesadilla

**Ingredients:**

- 4 large eggs
- 1/2 cup cheese (cheddar or your choice), shredded
- 1/4 cup cooked sausage or bacon (optional)
- 4 large tortillas
- Salt and pepper to taste
- Salsa for serving

**Instructions:**

1. In a bowl, whisk together eggs, salt, and pepper. Scramble the eggs in a skillet until cooked.
2. Place a tortilla in the skillet, sprinkle half with cheese, cooked eggs, and sausage or bacon if using. Fold the tortilla over.
3. Cook until golden brown on both sides and the cheese is melted.
4. Slice and serve with salsa.

## Egg and Cheese Scones

**Ingredients:**

- 2 cups all-purpose flour
- 1 tablespoon baking powder
- 1/2 teaspoon salt
- 1/2 cup cold butter, cubed
- 1 cup shredded cheese (cheddar or your choice)
- 1/2 cup milk
- 2 large eggs

**Instructions:**

1. Preheat the oven to 400°F (200°C) and line a baking sheet with parchment paper.
2. In a bowl, combine flour, baking powder, and salt. Cut in the cold butter until the mixture resembles coarse crumbs.
3. Stir in cheese. In a separate bowl, whisk together milk and eggs, then add to the dry ingredients, mixing until just combined.
4. Turn the dough onto a floured surface, shape into a circle, and cut into wedges. Place on the baking sheet and bake for 15-20 minutes until golden brown.

**Broccoli and Cheddar Quiche**

**Ingredients:**

- 1 pie crust (store-bought or homemade)
- 1 cup broccoli florets, chopped
- 1 cup shredded cheddar cheese
- 4 large eggs
- 1 cup milk
- Salt and pepper to taste

**Instructions:**

1. Preheat the oven to 375°F (190°C) and place the pie crust in a pie dish.
2. Blanch the broccoli in boiling water for 2-3 minutes, then drain.
3. In a bowl, whisk together eggs, milk, salt, and pepper.
4. Spread the broccoli and cheese evenly in the pie crust, then pour the egg mixture on top.
5. Bake for 30-35 minutes until the quiche is set and lightly golden. Allow to cool slightly before slicing.

**Egg and Potato Breakfast Skillet**

**Ingredients:**

- 4 large eggs
- 2 cups diced potatoes
- 1/2 cup bell peppers, diced
- 1/2 cup onion, diced
- 2 tablespoons olive oil
- Salt and pepper to taste

**Instructions:**

1. In a skillet, heat olive oil over medium heat. Add diced potatoes and cook until tender and golden brown, about 10-15 minutes.
2. Add bell peppers and onion, cooking until softened.
3. Create wells in the skillet and crack an egg into each well. Cover and cook until the eggs are set to your liking.
4. Season with salt and pepper before serving.

**Mediterranean Egg Bake**

**Ingredients:**

- 6 large eggs
- 1 cup cherry tomatoes, halved
- 1/2 cup feta cheese, crumbled
- 1/2 cup spinach, chopped
- 1/4 cup black olives, sliced
- Salt and pepper to taste

**Instructions:**

1. Preheat the oven to 375°F (190°C) and grease a baking dish.
2. In a bowl, whisk together eggs, salt, and pepper. Stir in tomatoes, feta, spinach, and olives.
3. Pour the mixture into the baking dish and bake for 25-30 minutes until set and golden.
4. Allow to cool slightly before slicing and serving.

## Egg-Stuffed Bell Peppers

**Ingredients:**

- 4 bell peppers, halved and seeds removed
- 8 large eggs
- 1/2 cup cheese (cheddar or your choice), shredded
- Salt and pepper to taste
- Fresh herbs for garnish (optional)

**Instructions:**

1. Preheat the oven to 375°F (190°C) and place bell pepper halves in a baking dish.
2. In a bowl, whisk together eggs, salt, and pepper. Stir in cheese.
3. Pour the egg mixture into each bell pepper half, filling them about 3/4 full.
4. Bake for 25-30 minutes until the eggs are set. Garnish with fresh herbs before serving.

Enjoy these delicious egg recipes!

## Spinach, Bacon, and Egg Salad

**Ingredients:**

- 4 large eggs, hard-boiled and chopped
- 4 cups fresh spinach, washed and dried
- 6 slices bacon, cooked and crumbled
- 1/2 cup cherry tomatoes, halved
- 1/4 red onion, thinly sliced
- 1/4 cup crumbled feta cheese
- 3 tablespoons olive oil
- 1 tablespoon red wine vinegar
- Salt and pepper to taste

**Instructions:**

1. In a large bowl, combine spinach, chopped eggs, crumbled bacon, cherry tomatoes, red onion, and feta cheese.
2. In a small bowl, whisk together olive oil, red wine vinegar, salt, and pepper. Drizzle over the salad and toss to combine.
3. Serve immediately.

## Crispy Eggplant and Egg Sandwich

**Ingredients:**

- 1 medium eggplant, sliced into rounds
- 2 large eggs
- 1 cup breadcrumbs
- 1/2 cup flour
- 1/2 teaspoon garlic powder
- Salt and pepper to taste
- Olive oil for frying
- 4 slices of bread
- Lettuce, tomato, and condiments for serving

**Instructions:**

1. Set up a breading station with flour, beaten eggs, and breadcrumbs mixed with garlic powder, salt, and pepper.
2. Dip eggplant slices in flour, then egg, and finally coat with breadcrumbs.
3. Heat olive oil in a skillet over medium heat. Fry eggplant slices until golden brown on both sides. Drain on paper towels.
4. Assemble sandwiches with eggplant, fried eggs, lettuce, and tomato on bread. Add condiments as desired.

**Caprese Egg Bake**

**Ingredients:**

- 6 large eggs
- 1 cup cherry tomatoes, halved
- 1 cup fresh mozzarella balls, halved
- 1/4 cup fresh basil, chopped
- Salt and pepper to taste
- Olive oil for greasing

**Instructions:**

1. Preheat the oven to 375°F (190°C) and grease a baking dish.
2. In a bowl, whisk together eggs, salt, and pepper. Stir in cherry tomatoes, mozzarella, and basil.
3. Pour the mixture into the greased baking dish and bake for 25-30 minutes until set and golden.
4. Allow to cool slightly before slicing and serving.

**Bacon-Wrapped Eggs**

**Ingredients:**

- 8 large eggs
- 8 slices of bacon
- Salt and pepper to taste
- Fresh herbs for garnish (optional)

**Instructions:**

1. Preheat the oven to 400°F (200°C) and grease a muffin tin.
2. Cook bacon in a skillet until slightly crispy but still pliable. Drain on paper towels.
3. Wrap each slice of bacon around the sides of the muffin tin, creating a nest.
4. Crack an egg into each bacon-wrapped cup. Season with salt and pepper.
5. Bake for 15-20 minutes until the eggs are cooked to your liking. Garnish with herbs if desired.

**Frittata with Roasted Vegetables**

**Ingredients:**

- 6 large eggs
- 1 cup mixed roasted vegetables (bell peppers, zucchini, onions, etc.)
- 1/2 cup cheese (feta, goat cheese, or your choice), crumbled
- 1/4 cup milk
- Salt and pepper to taste
- Olive oil for greasing

**Instructions:**

1. Preheat the oven to 375°F (190°C) and grease a baking dish or oven-safe skillet.
2. In a bowl, whisk together eggs, milk, salt, and pepper. Stir in roasted vegetables and cheese.
3. Pour the egg mixture into the greased dish and bake for 25-30 minutes until set and lightly golden.
4. Allow to cool slightly before slicing and serving.

## Egg Tacos with Salsa Verde

**Ingredients:**

- 4 large eggs
- 1/4 cup cheese (cheddar or your choice), shredded
- 4 small tortillas
- Salsa verde for topping
- Fresh cilantro for garnish (optional)
- Salt and pepper to taste

**Instructions:**

1. In a skillet, scramble the eggs with salt and pepper until cooked through. Stir in cheese until melted.
2. Warm the tortillas in a separate skillet or microwave.
3. Fill each tortilla with scrambled eggs and top with salsa verde.
4. Garnish with fresh cilantro if desired and serve warm.

## Egg and Cheese Breakfast Bowl

**Ingredients:**

- 4 large eggs
- 1 cup cooked quinoa or rice
- 1/2 cup cheese (cheddar or your choice), shredded
- 1/2 avocado, sliced
- Salt and pepper to taste
- Fresh herbs for garnish (optional)

**Instructions:**

1. In a skillet, scramble the eggs with salt and pepper until cooked through.
2. In bowls, layer cooked quinoa or rice, scrambled eggs, and cheese.
3. Top with sliced avocado and garnish with fresh herbs if desired.
4. Serve warm.

Enjoy these delicious and hearty egg recipes!

**Tomato and Egg Stir-Fry**

**Ingredients:**

- 4 large eggs
- 2 medium tomatoes, chopped
- 2 tablespoons vegetable oil
- 2 green onions, chopped
- Salt and pepper to taste
- 1 tablespoon soy sauce (optional)

**Instructions:**

1. In a bowl, whisk the eggs and season with salt and pepper.
2. Heat vegetable oil in a skillet over medium heat. Add chopped tomatoes and sauté until softened.
3. Push the tomatoes to the side and pour in the beaten eggs. Scramble gently until cooked through.
4. Add green onions and soy sauce, if using. Mix everything together and serve hot.

**Egg and Quinoa Breakfast Bowl**

**Ingredients:**

- 2 cups cooked quinoa
- 4 large eggs
- 1 cup spinach, sautéed
- 1/2 avocado, sliced
- 1/4 cup feta cheese, crumbled
- Salt and pepper to taste

**Instructions:**

1. In a skillet, cook the eggs to your liking (scrambled, poached, or fried).
2. In bowls, layer cooked quinoa, sautéed spinach, and eggs.
3. Top with sliced avocado and crumbled feta cheese. Season with salt and pepper to taste.

## Herb-Crusted Baked Eggs

**Ingredients:**

- 4 large eggs
- 1/2 cup breadcrumbs
- 1/4 cup grated Parmesan cheese
- 1 tablespoon fresh herbs (parsley, thyme, or your choice), chopped
- 2 tablespoons olive oil
- Salt and pepper to taste

**Instructions:**

1. Preheat the oven to 375°F (190°C) and grease a baking dish.
2. In a bowl, mix breadcrumbs, Parmesan cheese, herbs, olive oil, salt, and pepper.
3. Create wells in the breadcrumb mixture and crack an egg into each well.
4. Bake for 15-20 minutes until the eggs are set. Serve warm.

## Korean Gyeran-jjim (Steamed Eggs)

**Ingredients:**

- 4 large eggs
- 1/2 cup water or chicken broth
- Salt to taste
- 1 green onion, finely chopped
- Sesame oil for drizzling

**Instructions:**

1. In a bowl, whisk eggs with water or broth and salt until well combined.
2. Pour the mixture into a heatproof bowl or steamer dish.
3. Place the dish in a steamer and steam for 10-15 minutes until the eggs are fluffy and set.
4. Garnish with chopped green onion and a drizzle of sesame oil before serving.

## Eggs with Ratatouille

**Ingredients:**

- 4 large eggs
- 1 cup ratatouille (cooked mixture of eggplant, zucchini, bell peppers, and tomatoes)
- Olive oil for frying
- Salt and pepper to taste

**Instructions:**

1. In a skillet, heat olive oil over medium heat and add ratatouille. Cook until heated through.
2. Create wells in the ratatouille and crack an egg into each well.
3. Cover and cook until the eggs are set to your liking. Season with salt and pepper before serving.

## Cauliflower and Egg Casserole

**Ingredients:**

- 1 head cauliflower, chopped into florets
- 6 large eggs
- 1 cup milk
- 1 cup cheese (cheddar or your choice), shredded
- Salt and pepper to taste
- 1 teaspoon garlic powder

**Instructions:**

1. Preheat the oven to 375°F (190°C) and grease a baking dish.
2. Steam or microwave the cauliflower until tender, then spread in the baking dish.
3. In a bowl, whisk together eggs, milk, garlic powder, salt, and pepper. Pour over the cauliflower.
4. Sprinkle cheese on top and bake for 30-35 minutes until the eggs are set and the top is golden.

## Rustic Egg and Vegetable Tart

**Ingredients:**

- 1 sheet puff pastry, thawed
- 4 large eggs
- 1 cup mixed vegetables (bell peppers, onions, spinach, etc.), sautéed
- 1/2 cup cheese (feta, goat cheese, or your choice), crumbled
- Salt and pepper to taste

**Instructions:**

1. Preheat the oven to 400°F (200°C) and roll out the puff pastry on a floured surface to fit a tart pan.
2. Place the pastry in the tart pan and prick the bottom with a fork.
3. In a bowl, whisk together eggs, salt, and pepper. Stir in sautéed vegetables and cheese.
4. Pour the egg mixture into the pastry shell and bake for 25-30 minutes until the eggs are set and the pastry is golden. Allow to cool slightly before slicing and serving.

Enjoy these delightful egg recipes!

www.ingramcontent.com/pod-product-compliance
Lightning Source LLC
LaVergne TN
LVHW081336060526
838201LV00055B/2690